CW00556072

BIRMINGHAM
INTERNATIONAL
AIRPORT

Mike Vines

Airlife
England

Author's Profile

My interest in aviation and in Birmingham Airport started at the tender age of eight when I used to 'persuade' anyone who would listen to take me to watch the aeroplanes at Elmdon, as it was then. Now aged 48, I have achieved one of my long-held ambitions to produce a photographic book on Birmingham International Airport.

I started photographing aeroplanes with my box brownie from the age of about fourteen, and caught the bug for aviation photography. Seven years as a photographer/air observer for the British Ministry of Defence confirmed my aeroplane mania. I worked as a freelance aviation photographer in my spare time for many years and finally in 1990 took the plunge and formed my own company — Photo Link — specialising in aviation work. From my Birmingham base, the last twenty months have seen me in Louisiana, New York State, Florida, France and Romania on aviation photo assignments — and I always try to fly from Birmingham.

I currently use Nikon F.4 and F.3 35 mm format cameras and a Pentax 6 cm x 7 cm medium format for commercial, aerial and air-to-air work. This book was shot using my 35 mm camera and Fuji 100D and 400D transparency film.

The enthusiasm at Birmingham for this project started with the managing director Bob Taylor OBE, DL, who is an ex-RAF Gloster Meteor pilot.

Without his help I doubt whether this book would ever have been attempted. Everyone I came into contact with was most helpful during what turned out to be a very hectic shooting schedule against the clock and the British weather! But a few more individual thanks are a must.

To Sheila Lashford, head of external relations, and Rachel Coggan of the press and public relations office for arranging visits and passes. To operations duty manager Lyndon Griffiths, known as 'Duracell' for his incredible energy, thanks for letting me try to keep up with you during several busy twelve-hour shifts. But most of all, my special thanks to cargo development manager Ken Perks, known affectionately as Captain Cargo, without whose help this book would have been very hard work. He spent days away from his desk escorting me to every corner of the airport and then came back in the evenings, nights and weekends for more. He even made it to a 3 am photocall — and I didn't! But I still made it in time for dawn pictures, thanks to his wake-up call.

Grateful thanks also to Simon Morris of Dunn's Photographic Laboratories for his fast turnround service and consistency of film processing, and to Phil Goldsmith, branch manager of KJ&P Ltd, and Roger Wakefield of Shutterbugs Ltd, for the loan of specialist lenses.

Mike Vines

First published in the UK in 1991 by Airlife Publishing Ltd

British Library Cataloguing in Publication Data
A catalogue record for this book is available from the British Library.

ISBN 1 85310 318 7

Colour reproduction by Adroit Photo Litho Ltd, Cecil Street, Birmingham B19 3ST

Printed by Livesey Ltd, Shrewsbury

Airlife Publishing Ltd
101 Longden Road, Shrewsbury SY3 9EB

It gives me great pleasure to introduce this book on Birmingham International Airport — or BHX as the airlines know us — during the year in which we opened our second exciting and innovative terminal, Eurohub.

The Airport has grown considerably since its opening in July 1939 and, some fifty-two years later, is now fifth in the UK Airports League and handling a growing number of passengers, presently around 3.6 million. Sixty per cent of these are travelling on scheduled services which increasingly serve the capital cities and main business centres of Scandinavia and Europe, the strong charter market stretching as far afield as Florida, Cyprus and the Canary Islands.

Operating on a 24-hour basis throughout the year, we are constantly building our network of services in order to provide the Midlands of the United Kingdom with a major gateway which also gives immediate access to the business opportunities and partnerships that now prevail within Europe. Over 4500 people presently work at the Airport for more than 100 companies and, as can be seen from many of the splendid photographs that appear in this book, the teamwork in order to provide safe, secure and efficient services needs to be always of a very high order.

I hope you will not only find enjoyment in reading about us, but will also visit the Airport and travel through here whenever possible.

R. R. Taylor
Managing Director

Above: Concorde at Eurohub.

Opposite: Sir Colin Marshall, Deputy Chairman and Chief Executive of British Airways, and Mr Bob Taylor, OBE, DL, managing director of Birmingham International Airport and the Chairman of Eurohub plc. British Airways Concorde 102 G-BOAD flew in for the first operational day of the £60 million Eurohub on 22 July 1991.

Introduction

Birmingham Airport (Elmdon) was opened on 8 July 1939, and by the time Birmingham International Airport celebrated its 50th anniversary in 1989 it was the fifth largest airport in the UK in terms of total passenger throughput, and the tenth largest in terms of flown cargo. Soon after its official opening in 1939, Elmdon Airport was requisitioned for the duration of the Second World War and not officially handed back to the City of Birmingham until 1960.

But post-war scheduled services started in 1949 with a British European Airways service to Paris and, with the start of inclusive package tours six years later, the airport really started to hum.

In 1967 the main runway was extended, and by the early 1970s over a million passengers a year were using the airport and what was becoming an overcrowded terminal building. Finally, after many alterations and extensions to the terminal, the move from the west side of the airport to a new purpose-built £62 million terminal building was made in 1984. With its unique Maglev (Magnetic Levitation) people mover linking it in just ninety seconds to the National Exhibition Centre and a rail link at Birmingham International station, it provided a much-needed upgrade for Birmingham International Airport.

The move also opened up the opportunity for concentrating cargo handling on the now vacated site of the old terminal building and British Airways opened their purpose-built cargo centre in 1986. Leading names in the express parcel market have now brought the 'original (Elmdon) terminal' back to life, and currently over 2000 metric tonnes of cargo is flown in and out of Birmingham a month. The 'original terminal' is still also home to Air Traffic Control.

The popularity of the new passenger terminal with travellers, and the increased destinations offered by the new scheduled and inclusive tour airlines was reflected in Birmingham's 1989/90 figures when 3.5 million passengers used BHX (Birmingham's International code).

Now there is Eurohub, a £60 million investment in the future of the airport and the Birmingham area. From the initial 'back of envelope' sketches to the opening on 22 July 1991, this new terminal was achieved in just thirty-three months. It is the world's first integrated domestic and international airline 'hub' terminal designed to provide dedicated facilities to support British Airways, Birmingham European Airways and Caledonian Airways, and will enable the airport to handle around seven million passengers a year through the two terminals.

Opposite: February 1991 and it's −5°C with a wind chill factor making it more like −14°C, but Birmingham's snow clearers have worked throughout the night to clear the runways and taxiways.

Below: Ground operations Land-Rover, call sign Mobile 7, waits at airfield checkpoint Bravo while a recently-landed British Airways BAC One-Eleven heads for the warmth of the terminal.

Opposite: A Caledonian Airways Lockheed Tri-Star applies reverse thrust as it diverts into Birmingham from Munich. Heavy snow storms were still raging over the south-east and its home base of Gatwick was closed.

Below: It's 07.35 and Swissair flight SR 867 in the shape of a McDonnell Douglas MD-81 taxies to the holding point for runway one-five before departure to Zurich. This morning the aircraft is HB-INU, and just visible behind the Swiss machine is a BEA BAC One-Eleven.

Opposite: Early morning on the apron, and as the mist starts to dissipate, the whine of jet engines running-up heralds the start of another busy day.

An Air 2000 Boeing 757 inches its way forward on to the threshold of runway three-three. Air 2000 currently operate twelve of these sleek Boeings, seven of them being the EROPS (Extended Range Operations) versions.

Below: Air Foyle operates a fleet of British Aerospace (BAe) 146–200 and 300QT (Quiet Transport) for the overnight express cargo carrier TNT. This aircraft, in TNT livery, is a 200QT version and is Prestwick bound for the last leg of its overnight flight from Cologne.

Opposite: International freight from Cologne is unloaded just after dawn from TNT's BAe 146–200QT. Up to three pallets are rolled on to the Hi-Lo loader, which then descends so that they can be rolled on to dollies. The pallets will be unloaded and sorted in the TNT cargo terminal, where a fleet of road vehicles will deliver them to their final destinations.

The Express
TNT 0030
TNT
There's always a plane near you
TNT Express Europe
TNT
Birmingham International Airport
KEEP CLEAR

Below: Birmingham is the UK import hub for Emery Worldwide, and here Karen Smith (foreground), Julie Allison (centre) and Jackie Vasey input information into the central computer. Emery use Channel Express's Handley Page Heralds from Birmingham to their European hub in Maastricht, Holland, where the cargo is transferred to long-range aircraft bound for the United States.

Opposite: United Parcels Service driver Nigel Mascall, complete with baseball cap and lacking only an American accent, helps the loaders sort parcels into the correct pallets for tonight's load out of Birmingham, bound for UPS's European hub in Cologne. From there they will connect with flights to their US hub in Louisville, Kentucky.

Below: Not the inside of the Channel tunnel, but the interior of Airbridge Carriers' Lockheed L-188CF Electra, F-OGST. Its 76.5 ft main cabin will carry eight 88 in x 108 in pallets and two smaller ones, and under the floor it can also carry another 3000 kilos — making a total of 15,450 kilos which can be carried non-stop for up to 1000 miles.

Opposite: Pictured in TNT's cargo shed loading pallets, already on their wheeled trailers, is load bay operator Bob Heir. This pallet is for Cologne and will be flown out in a TNT BAe 146.

Below: 07.45 and Airbridge's 'French' Electra is back from Cologne and on finals for runway three-three. The ground handlers are ready and waiting on the apron to unload its cargo with all possible speed.

Opposite: Airbridge's freighter, a Lockheed L-188CF Electra, F-OGST, disgorges its pallets. The aircraft is currently leased from Servicios De Transportes Aereos Fueguinos of Argentina and is flown by a mix of British and Argentinian aircrews, with an American and Argentinian groundcrew. The original 1939 terminal building in the background still houses Air Traffic Control (ATC) and offers attractive office space for rent.

Below: The Electra has been pushed back with two of its 4000 hp Allison turbo props already turning and the others just starting — now, with all four turning, the pilots are ready to follow the green taxiway lights to the runway. Around 180 Electras were built and over 100 of them are still flying as freighters. F-OGST first flew in 1959 as an L-188c with Qantas as VH-ECA, then with Air California in 1967 as N359AC and Ecuatoriana in 1971 as HC-AVX. It was converted to a freighter (L-188CF) in 1976, was then operated by LACSA as TI-LRM, then registered to James B. Qually until 1987 as N359Q, and finally to its current Argentinian owners in 1987.

Opposite: Morning is breaking as a Birmingham European Airways BAC One-Eleven is readied for its first trip of the day. BEA has five BAC One-Eleven 400 series aircraft and will be re-introducing its three BAe Jetstreams from October 1991 instead of its current two Shorts SD3–60s.

Below: This Flanders Airlines Fokker F 27 Friendship series 100 was captained by Californianborn Carl Kennedy and was hauling 500 kilos of live eels from Lough Neagh in Northern Ireland. After picking up more cargo in Birmingham, where OO-SVM was only on the ground for forty-five minutes, it headed off for its final leg to Brussels.

Opposite: A Short SD3–60 of Manx Airlines climbs out on its way back to the Isle of Man with a full load of thirty-six passengers on board. These unpressurised short-haulers are known affectionately as 'sheds' because of their boxy fuselages; this particular variant, with its single fin, is known as a super shed.

Below: Call-sign Swissair eight-six-seven, a McDonnell Douglas MD-81 taxies towards the threshold of runway one-five for departure to Zurich.

Opposite: The morning rush-hour and a BEA, BAC One-Eleven waits for clearance on to runway three-three after the departing British Airways BAC One-Eleven. BEA's radio call-sign is Birmex, and here Birmex four-zero-five's crew waits to launch-off to Belfast.

Below: The business-like interior of the new £60 million Eurohub is readied for its July 22 opening. It is the second terminal opened at Birmingham within the last seven years. Used exclusively by British Airways, Birmingham European and Caledonian Airways, the hub has sixteen check-in desks, touch-screen ticket dispensers and ten air-bridges. It is the first purpose-built hub terminal in Europe.

Opposite: Arriving from Jersey, an Air UK BAe 146–200, G-CHSR, is on finals as it bleeds-off some speed with its rear air-brakes extended before a smooth landing on runway three-three.

Opposite main picture: A Humber Monoplane non-flyable replica hangs from the ceiling in the main terminal.

Opposite inserts: Passenger amenities including two branches of W H Smith, boutiques, a hobby shop, Aviator Bar and the Duty Free shop in Eurohub.

Right: To the traveller, one of the most important pieces of kit is the baggage trolley. Bill Butler (L. H.) and Keith Simpson are part of the ground operations team which helps to keep things moving. Pictured in the main terminal, they could also find themselves baggage and freight handling out on the apron.

Below: British Airways operate thirteen BAC One-Eleven series 500 out of Birmingham to destinations all over the UK and Europe. The series 500 was first flown in 1967 and although British production finished with the series 475 in 1970, Rombac of Romania is still producing One-Elevens in Bucharest and the Dee Howard Corporation in the US are fitting the new generation Rolls-Royce Tay turbofans to these strong airframes.

Opposite: A Toronto-bound Nationair Boeing 757–28A (EROPS) lifts off very quickly with 228 passengers aboard and full fuel tanks. This aircraft is powered by two Rolls-Royce RB211–535 E4 Turbofans which, because of their incredible reliability, have been cleared for extended range over water and uninhabited areas. Previously to operate for any length of time over these kind of areas an aircraft had to be fitted with three or four engines. My guide and mentor, Ken Perks, took this take-off shot while I was heading for Düsseldorf aboard a BA BAC One-Eleven to take the shot on pages 68/69.

Below: Air traffic services assistant Joe Wragg of the CAA (Civil Aviation Authority) Flight Briefing Unit gives the latest flight information to pilot Kim Knight (L. H.) of the Warwickshire Aero Centre, who is about to take his Commercial and Instructor's Licence. All the latest NOTAMS (Notice to Airmen), including possible delays, Purple Airspace (Royal Flights) and the latest weather reports will be part of the briefing. After gaining his licence, Kim will train pilots up to Private Pilot's Licence standard at Birmingham.

Opposite: British Airways pilots head for their office; a BAC One-Eleven. They are bound for Paris.

Below: Although painted in the Air France colour scheme, this Fokker F-28 Fellowship 4000 is in fact owned by Transport Aerien Transregional and is operated on behalf of Air France on some of its Paris Charles de Gaulle-Birmingham service.

Opposite: A TAT Fokker F-28 Fellowship 4000, F-GDFC, is replenished for its return flight to Paris, while a BEA BAC One-Eleven taxies out past Eurohub on its mid-morning flight to Amsterdam.

Below: Looking bronzed from a couple of weeks in the Bulgarian sunshine, holidaymakers pour off a Tupolev TU-154.

Opposite: A Balkan Bulgarian Tupolev TU-154B-2, LZ-BTT, gets the OK from the ground engineer that push-back is complete and the Russian-designed three 'holer' is ready to taxi out for departure to Varna.

Below: A TAT F-28 Fellowship 1000, F-GBBT, is readied for push-back from its stand. The ground engineer is in contact with the flight crew and awaits their clearance to pull out the ground power supply cable and check that the aircraft is clear of ground obstacles before it can safely move back under the power of the tug.

Opposite: Framed with runway three-three's approach lights, an Air 2000 Boeing 757 slides down the glideslope.

Below: The MAGLEV (Magnetic Levitation) system has been in operation ever since the main terminal was opened in 1984, moving passengers in ninety seconds from the Airport to Birmingham International rail station and the National Exhibition Centre. In the background is the walkway connecting the main terminal to the Novotel.

Opposite: Two British Airways BAC One-Elevens wait at Eurohub.

Below: Midland Airport Services staff check-in passengers for the Cyprus Airways flight CY 439 to Larnaca.

Opposite: Security checks are an ever-present necessity for today's air traveller. I can vouch for the fact that the Rapiscan machine, left, is safe for film up to a speed of 1000 ASA, and holiday films are usually of 100 ASA, so have no fear, your snaps won't be affected. Hand baggage searches are standard these days too, because of the need for maximum security.

Below: Spanish inclusive tour operator Oasis International Airlines operates a fleet of McDonnell Douglas MD-83s, but this newly-registered machine, EC-793 (793 is a temporary registration), is believed to be an MD-82. It is pictured here arriving from Malaga.

Opposite: Off to the sunshine — passengers board an Airtours McDonnell Douglas MD-83. The ground power supply is still connected to the aircraft in the foreground.

Below: A holidaymaker's surf board is loaded on to a Britannia Airways Boeing 767 bound for Orlando.

Opposite: Britannia's Boeing 767 wide-body leads an Air 2000 Boeing 757 narrow-body out to the taxiway and departure from runway one-five.

Right: Birmingham European Airways engineers check the APU (Auxiliary Power Unit) on one of their BAC One-Eleven 400 series aircraft. In the background is a BEA Short SD3–60 commuter airliner.

Below: The Britannia Airways Boeing 767 fin dwarfs two of the smaller Boeing 737s and a BEA BAC One-Eleven.

Opposite: Apron controllers, Grant Platts (L.H.) and Barrie Pickett have the best view in the house, or at least as good as Air Traffic Control on the opposite side of the airport. Here they are keeping their eyes on Royal Flight, BAe 146-C1 'Kittyhawk 4' (centre, top) as it taxies in to pick up the Prince of Wales. Their official title is airfield operations assistants and their tasks also include marshalling and bird-scaring, when they operate from radio-equipped Land-Rovers. But today, 120 feet up in their tower, they are responsible for the allocation of airliner stands.

Below: Ossie, an Irish Water Spaniel, is sniffing for drugs under the supervision of his H.M. Customs and Excise handler Michael Butler. There are two dogs based at BHX. Owned by the Royal Air Force, they are leased to Customs and Excise. Home is a 'doggy Hilton' purpose-built kennel, and the dogs are rigorously inspected by a vet every month. According to Customs men, the dogs are the most effective and fastest way of checking baggage and freight for illegal drugs.

Opposite: A BEA BAC One-Eleven and a Short SD3–60 lead a British Airways BAe (Hawker Siddeley) 748 out to the threshold of runway three-three. The 748s, which are affectionately known as 'Budgies' by their crews, operate the Birmingham to Aberdeen and Edinburgh routes.

Below: Looking at the screen over air traffic controller Nick Crawford's shoulder. Each blip is an aircraft and most of them have a four-digit number attached for instant aircraft identification. Nick is operating on frequency 131.32. Have you ever listened on an air band radio and heard the controller tell the airline pilot to squawk with a series of numbers? The pilot will then dial in these numbers on his transponder box and that number stays with the aircraft blip until completion of the flight. The area in the centre of the screen is the Birmingham Air Traffic Control zone, and each circle on the screen is twenty miles in diameter, so Nick is looking at a maximum range of sixty miles at the edge of his screen.

Opposite: Under the glass-house in Air Traffic Control sit the three-man radar room team. Air traffic controllers Nick Crawford (L.H.) and Phido Howard in the middle co-ordinating seat, with air traffic services assistant John Riddell. Aircraft arriving from or going to the south are received from or handed over to the London Air Traffic Control Centre, and from the north are handled by a sub centre at Manchester.

Below: This Airbridge Carriers Vickers V 953 Merchantman freighter has been pushed back and the despatcher is checking the away-time. This machine, registration G-APEJ, and named AJAX, is now one of five operated by Airbridge, who are retiring one Merchantman a year and replacing them with Electras and Boeing 727s.

Opposite: Sergeant David Storr is one of five Sergeant Observers attached to the Police Air Operations Unit based at BHX. The many extras in the cockpit of this specially kitted out Aerospatiale AS 355F-2 Twin Squirrel include a thermal image camera, a 30,000,000 candle power night sun light and a 700 watt Skyshout loud-hailer system. On the left of the cockpit is the observer's screen, showing the picture taken by the thermal image camera. The pictures are beamed to police HQ as they are taken.

Below: Constable John Plant of the West Midlands Airport Police Unit worked the beat outside the airport for twenty-three years, and has been on the inside for the last seven years. John is a total aviation person. He gained his private pilot's licence in 1983 and has now notched up about 125 hours flying time. If there was an emergency at the airport, John or one of his colleagues could be one of the first people to meet up with outside emergency personnel.

Opposite: This Short Skyvan 3 freighter of Danish Air Transport, based at Billund, is as its name implies, a flying van. It was waiting at Birmingham for a consignment of 1000 kilos of satellite dishes to arrive. Pictured here is Birmingham Airport's cargo development manager, Ken Perks, talking to co-pilot Thomas Jacobsen.

Right: Outside the main terminal building is this beautiful birds in flight metal sculpture. In the background is the connecting walkway between the main terminal and the Birmingham Airport Novotel.

Bottom: The Right Hon the Earl of Aylesford, Lord Lieutenant of the West Midlands, introduces the Princess of Wales to Mr Bob Taylor, OBE, DL, the managing director of Birmingham International Airport.

Opposite: A Queen's Flight BAe 146 Cl with Royal Standard flying brings the Princess of Wales on an official visit to the West Midlands. The Queen's Flight operates three of these quiet airliners.

EUROHUB

BIRMINGHAM

Below: Aurigny Air Services operate this very pretty thirty-six seater Short SD3–60 on its new Birmingham to Jersey route.

Opposite: A Cessna 320, a Cessna 152 and a Piper Navajo parked beneath Air Traffic Control on the general aviation ramp.

Below: City Hopper, which is a sister company of KLM (Royal Dutch Airlines), operates four different types of aircraft on its Amsterdam-Birmingham service. Here a thirty-three seat Saab 340B taxies to the main terminal.

Opposite: An Air 2000 Boeing 757 crew waits for their 233 passengers to arrive before flying out to Heraklion in Crete.

Below: A Lufthansa Boeing 737–230 arrives from Frankfurt. In the background is the fuel farm near the threshold to runway three-three.

Opposite: British Airways Birmingham flight manager, Captain David Lusher (L.H.) and his co-pilot, First Officer Rob Meyers, start the descent into Birmingham from Düsseldorf. Our BAC One-Eleven's callsign for this return leg is Speedbird 5381, and our total time from chocks-off at Birmingham to our return was just three hours and ten minutes, with just thirty minutes on the ground in Germany. This wasn't the end of the day for the flight crew and the four cabin crew of G-AXLL though, as they then prepared to fly to Edinburgh.

Below Left: An airport loader drives back on to the apron for another load of baggage from the Cyprus Airways Airbus A310.

Below Centre: Spanish scheduled carrier Iberia operates McDonnell Douglas MD-87s and Douglas DC-9s into Birmingham from Madrid and Barcelona. Here an MD-87 heads from taxiway one to the threshold of runway one-five.

Overleaf: Dan Air flight DA 2463 in the shape of a Boeing 737–200 series aircraft is about to touch British soil again after its flight from Malaga.

Below: As well as passengers, the Cyprus Airways Airbus A 310 brings in a lot of freight in its under-floor hold. Today a huge consignment of grapes is unloaded, and the Birmingham Airport loader is checking that the strapping is safe before loading it on to a road vehicle for delivery.

Opposite: Cyprus Airways 5B-DAR is an Airbus Industrie A 310–203, which is being turned around at breakneck speed; normally ground handlers, refuellers and cleaners have a maximum of seventy minutes to complete their tasks, but today with air traffic delays caused over Europe, the team have only fifty minutes to turn round this 241-seat wide-body.

Below: Shell UK Oil airfield operator Roy Evans checks his hose connectors in the underwing points on a Cyprus Airways Airbus A 310. Aviation fuel is pumped aboard the aircraft at the phenomenal rate of 1,650 litres per minute, and a total of 25,928 litres was pumped aboard the aircraft on this occasion. Shell, Esso and BP are all based at the fuel farm at the south end of Birmingham International Airport.

Opposite: This ex-Brymon Airways De Havilland Dash 7 – 102 series machine is now operated by British Midland and is painted in an interim livery before a full respray will show it in the company's colours of blue and red.

Below: Jersey European Airway's Fokker F 27 Friendship 500 series flies in from Belfast City Airport. As their name implies, the airline flies to Jersey, and Guernsey as well.

Opposite: Lockheed Electra freighter, F-OGST, gets some attention to its number one Allison turboprop engine from one of its American ground crew members during its down-time in the day.

Below: British Airways engineers get to grips with an engine change on this BAC One-Eleven 500 series aircraft in the BA engineering hangar. The engine is a Rolls-Royce Spey 512 and, as Alan Lang, British Airways station maintenance manager, explained: 'A complete engine change takes about sixteen to eighteen hours, including ground test running.' Sixty-six BA engineers are based at Birmingham, working five shifts, twenty-four hours a day, seven days a week. Pictured here are (bottom, left to right) Mark Thompson, Steve Urwin-Mann, Dave Morris and Joe Brown.

Opposite: A British Midland Airways, Douglas DC-9-14 on arrival frames Birmingham International's terminals.

Below: An Irish Air Corps, BAe 125-700B executive jet brings in VIPs to a meeting in the vicinity.

Opposite: The smallest scheduled airliner flying into Birmingham is this eight-seater Piper PA-42 Cheyenne III belonging to BASE Business Airlines of the Netherlands. This brand new service was introduced from Eindhoven to Birmingham during the shooting of this book. Business was so good after the first few days that the service was operated by a nineteen-seat BAe Jetstream 31 from then on.

Below: A Scandinavian Airlines System (SAS) Douglas DC-9 climbs out en-route to Copenhagen.

Opposite: A Cessna Citation executive jet belonging to Birmingham-based Eurojet is framed by a rainbow as a summer storm passes through. The main terminal is virtually blotted out by the intense squall.

Below: The in-flight caterers for every airline that operates out of Birmingham is Forte Airport Services. 9,500 meals a day are produced in their purpose-built temperature-controlled building. Forte at Birmingham spend £2.8 million a year on food purchasing, but their computerised costings are worked out to the nearest halfpence. In this shot, meals are being prepared in the cold kitchen for a Lufthansa flight which has ninety-eight business and twenty-eight economy passengers aboard.

Opposite: Air France shares the Birmingham-Paris route with British Airways. Some of the French flights are operated by TAT F 28 Fellowships, but depending on demand, anything from an Air France Boeing 727–200 to an Airbus A 320 is used. The service today is operated by an Air France Boeing 737–228.

Below: Peter Morgan (L.H.), duty engineering officer, and Roland Draper, general manager of Air Traffic Services, check out the Instrument Runway Visual Range Mk III, or IRVR; the structures are commonly known as Daleks. A light source is projected from one Dalek to the other and measured through a prism on to a receiver plate. When mist or fog forms, it is immediately read off on a duplicate instrument in Air Traffic Control, so that landing aircraft get the latest and most accurate poor visibility information from the three pairs of Daleks strategically placed alongside the runway.

Opposite: The national airline of Yugoslavia is JAT or Jugoslovenski Aerotransport, and pictured here is a Boeing 727-H9 on arrival on a scheduled service from Dubrovnik.

Below: Down at the Fire Station, which borders taxiway one, is a great place for visiting schoolchildren to wave to the pilots as they taxi to the runway. Judging from my visit, every pilot waved back to these budding pilots and cabin staff of the future.

Opposite: Charles Barton, visitors' facilities manager, explains how the airport works to visiting schoolchildren from Holbrook Primary School in Coventry. The most popular place is always the Fire Station, whether it's a children's tour or one organised for adults.

Below: Sister 'Timmi' Timmins is one of six sisters operating the Airport medical centre around the clock, and here she is conducting an audiometric (hearing) test on a new employee who is inside the soundproof booth.

Opposite: Yugoslavian tour operators Aviogenex are regular visitors to the airport, and on this particular arrival the Boeing 737 is greeted by some local birds on the approach.

Below: Air Malta's Boeing 737 slows down before turning left off the runway.

Opposite: The baggage hold of this 172-seat Air UK Leisure Boeing 737-42C, just in from Faro, is opened ready for unloading.

Below: A British-registered Trans European Airways Boeing 737–300 series launches from runway one-five.

Opposite: You can't start 'em young enough! Three-year-old Andrew Burckett was visiting the spectators' gallery with his granny, who admitted that she knew nothing about aeroplanes, so Richard Gabb, who was just passing, decided to lend a helping hand. With its hobbies shop and cafe, the spectators' gallery is very popular, and nearly 300,000 people a year pay to watch the aircraft from this vantage point.

Below: German airline DLT's Fokker 50 taxies to the terminal. What does DLT stand for? Are you sure you want to know? Well here goes — Deutsche Luftverkehrsgesellschaft.

Opposite: Canada 3000 Airlines' Boeing 757–28A makes ridiculously short work of take-off on its way to Toronto.

Below: An Aer Lingus Fokker 50 takes to the air with its nose wheel still retracting. These aircraft, which look very much like their predecessors, the Fokker Friendships, are fitted with the new generation Pratt & Whitney turboprops driving six-bladed propellers. This makes for a much quieter aeroplane.

Opposite: An Aer Lingus Fokker 50, a British Midland DC-9 and a British Airways BAC One-Eleven wait for their passengers.

Below: City Hopper's Fokker 50 quietly negotiates the apron, looking for its stand. The man-made mound behind the aircraft is called an earth bund and was built to cut down noise to the airport's neighbours.

Opposite: A full complement of eighteen business passengers had checked in for the evening flight to Eindhoven on this BAe Jetstream 31 of BASE Business Airlines of the Netherlands.

Below Left: This purpose-built metal tube, pressure-fed with aviation fuel (AVTUR) and atomised with air, generates a pretty realistic practice aircraft engine fire. Each fireman has to experience a live fire practice once a month, as well as a breathing apparatus check in the special smoke room in the Fire Station. The Civil Aviation Authority licences the airport and the Airport Fire Service annually.

Below Right: White Watch of Birmingham International Airport's Fire Service proudly pose for a dusk photograph in front of their purpose-built fire station. These thirty-ton foam tenders can produce 1,000 plus gallons of foam per minute. The Airport Fire Service consists of four watches (blue, white, red and green) each with 14 members. In total the Fire Service employs 62 people, including 5 watchroom attendants.

Opposite: A Balkan Bulgarian Airlines Tupolev TU-154B-2 lifts elegantly from runway one-five on an evening flight to Varna.

Below: An Airtours McDonnell Douglas MD-83, only a split-second from touch-down.

Opposite: An Adria Airways Douglas DC-9 brings back lucky holidaymakers from a full holiday in Pula. Why lucky? All of the passengers who went out on the next flight to Pula were to return only the following day because of the civil unrest in Yugoslavia.

Below: An Air 2000 Boeing 757, trailing vapour from its wings, on final approach to runway three-three.

Opposite: A TNT BAe 146-200 Quiet Trader taxies, under the marshaller's guidance, to its freight stand with a maximum load of 10.5 tonnes aboard.

Below: A Handley Page Dart Herald operated by Channel Express is loaded with Emery Worldwide freight before its night-flight to Maastricht, their European hub.

Opposite: The parcels conveyor belt goes right into the freight fuselage of this Fed Ex Fokker F 27 Friendship, which perhaps should be re-named a 'Freightship'.

Below: The Midlands media are anxious to gain first-hand accounts from holidaymakers back just one day after the start of their holiday in Yugoslavia. They were hurriedly brought home because of the potential civil war. For the airport's press and public relations department, this means that press facilities have to be laid on and controlled to cause minimum inconvenience to other air travellers and to the passengers concerned.

Opposite: A McDonnell Douglas MD-87 of CTA (Compagnie de Transport Aerien) taxies along taxiway five, ahead of a darkening sky. This Swiss aircraft, HB-IUA, is operating the Zurich flight for its parent company, Swissair.

Below: A Federal Express Fokker F 27 Friendship waits for its final load at sunset.

Opposite: This Swissair McDonnell Douglas MD-81 is parked for its overnight stop at Birmingham. In the morning it will operate the 07.40 service back to Zurich.

Below: Against a golden sky, a Jersey European Airways Fokker F 27 Friendship makes its final approach to runway one-five.

Opposite: The West Midlands Police Air Operations Unit's Twin Squirrel arrives back at its eastern apron landing pad at sunset. It is flown on night operations as well as by day. Its minimum height over the city at night is restricted to 600 feet instead of the 300 feet in daylight. The three pilots employed at the moment are ex-Army Air Corps, ex-RAF and ex-Royal Navy.

Below: A night stopping British Midland Douglas DC-9 and a BEA BAC One-Eleven are framed by the under-nose of a CAT MD-87.

Opposite: A Vickers V 953C Merchantman, named 'AJAX', waits for its 18.5 tonne pallet load to arrive before flying off to Brussels at 22.40.

Below: Iona National Airways' Embraer Bandeirante has just arrived from Dublin, operating the Federal Express overnight parcels service. A few hours on the ground and the two-man crew will be heading back to Dublin with parcels picked up from all over the country.

Opposite: A Cessna 500 Citation executive jet, G-TEFH, operated by Birmingham Aviation Ltd, gets a shower.

Below: Birmingham's two terminals are just across the main runway, but the streaks in the sky are the departing Airbridge Lockheed Electra, photographed with a four-second time exposure.